American 'Independent Automakers

Automakers

AMC to Willys 1945 to1960

Those were the days ... ™

VELOCE

Also from Veloce –

Those Were The Days ... Series
Alpine Trials & Rallies 1910-1973 (Pfundner)
American 'Independent' Automakers – AMC to Willys 1945 to 1960 (Mort)
American Station Wagons – The Golden Era 1950-1975 (Mort)
American Trucks of the 1950s (Mort)
American Trucks of the 1960s (Mort)
American Woodies 1928-1953 (Mort)
Anglo-American Cars from the 1930s to the 1970s (Mort)
Austerity Motoring (Bobbitt)
Austins, The last real (Peck)
Brighton National Speed Trials (Gardiner)
British Lorries of the 1950s (Bobbitt)
British Lorries of the 1960s (Bobbitt)
British Touring Car Racing (Collins)
British Police Cars (Walker)
British Woodies (Peck)
Café Racer Phenomenon, The (Walker)
Dune Buggy Phenomenon, The (Hale)
Dune Buggy Phenomenon Volume 2, The (Hale)
Endurance Racing at Silverstone in the 1970s & 1980s (Parker)
Hot Rod & Stock Car Racing in Britain in the 1980s (Neil)
Last Real Austins 1946-1959, The (Peck)
MG's Abingdon Factory (Moylan)
Motor Racing at Brands Hatch in the Seventies (Parker)
Motor Racing at Brands Hatch in the Eighties (Parker)
Motor Racing at Crystal Palace (Collins)
Motor Racing at Goodwood in the Sixties (Gardiner)
Motor Racing at Nassau in the 1950s & 1960s (O'Neil)
Motor Racing at Oulton Park in the 1960s (McFadyen)

Motor Racing at Oulton Park in the 1970s (McFadyen)
Superprix – The Story of Birmingham Motor Race (Page & Collins)
Three Wheelers (Bobbitt)

From Veloce Publishing's new imprints:

Soviet General & field rank officer uniforms: 1955 to 1991 (Streather)
Red & Soviet military & paramilitary services: female uniforms 1941-1991 (Streather)

Complete Dog Massage Manual, The – Gentle Dog Care (Robertson)
Dinner with Rover (Paton-Ayre)
Dog Games – Stimulating play to entertain your dog and you (Blenski)
Dog Relax – Relaxed dogs, relaxed owners (Pilguj)
Excercising your puppy: a gentle & natural approach (Robertson)
Know Your Dog – The guide to a beautiful relationship (Birmelin)
Living with an Older Dog – Gentle Dog Care (Alderton & Hall)
My dog is blind – but lives life to the full! (Horsky)
Smellorama – nose games for dogs (Theby)
Swim to Recovery: The Animal Magic Way (Wong)
Waggy Tails & Wheelchairs (Epp)
Winston ... the dog who changed my life (Klute)
You and Your Border Terrier – The Essential Guide (Alderton)
You and Your Cockapoo – The Essential Guide (Alderton)

www.veloce.co.uk

First published in June 2010 by Veloce Publishing Limited, Veloce House, Parkway Farm Business Park, Middle Farm Way, Poundbury, Dorchester, Dorset, DT1 3AR, England.
Fax 01305 250479/e-mail info@veloce.co.uk/web www.veloce.co.uk or www.velocebooks.com.
ISBN: 978-1-845842-39-0 UPC: 6-36847-04239-4
Readers with ideas for automotive books, or books on other transport or related hobby subjects, are invited to write to the editorial director of Veloce Publishing at the above address.
British Library Cataloguing in Publication Data – A catalogue record for this book is available from the British Library. Typesetting, design and page make-up all by Veloce Publishing Ltd on Apple Mac. Printed in India by Replika Press.

Contents

Preface

This is the sixth book written in conjunction with my son, Andrew, whose photographic skills help reveal the dramatic jet age styling and color of these designs built by the independent American automakers following WWII. Today, it is this 'flair' that makes these unique vehicles so appealing to collectors.

As well as my enthusiasm and fascination with the vehicles built by the American independent manufactures, and my son Andrew's photographic talents, this book would not have been possible without the encouragement, kindness and co-operation of many.

Rare Studebaker advertisements and a 1956 Studebaker Commander were provided through the kindness of Norm McWaters. Other Studebaker owners included Brendan McGrevy with his '55 Commander, and the stylish '56 President Pinehurst Station Wagon of Normand Gautreau.

The rare 1954 Willys of Dave Baker; Packards of Bruce Statton (1953 Mayfair) and Ron Dancey (1948 Custom and 1955 Caribbean); the Hudsons of Bob Kew (1955 Wasp), Arthur Caplan (1956 Hornet) and Ken Beselaere (1949 Brougham Coupe) were fine additions, as was the example of a 1947 Frazer kindly provided by Glen Woodcock.

Thanks too, for the fine examples of two Nash models each supplied by Mark Conforzi (Ramblers) and Chris Whillans (Statesman Sedans), as well as James Dilworth's 1954 Metropolitan.

We also appreciate the continued support of Hyman Motors Ltd, who kindly supplied numerous images of some very rare vehicles, and Legendary Motor Car in Canada.

Finally, both Andrew and I would like to thank Rod Grainger for his continued support and encouragement in writing this latest addition to Veloce Publishing's popular Those Were the Days ... series.

The 1950s would see the sun set on most of America's independent automakers, while even surviving Studebaker and AMC (Nash-Hudson) would both undergo a dramatic metamorphosis by the end of the decade.
(Courtesy Andrew Mort)

Introduction

Although General Motors, Ford and Chrysler had large volume and full model ranges, the remaining independent automakers who had survived the depression of the 1930s had the flexibility and enough capital from building planes, tanks, trucks, Jeeps, etc to launch new models for a car-starved North America following WWII. So lucrative was the American post-war car market that new automobile companies were also formed to cash in on the pent-up demand.

'American Independent Automakers 1945-1960,' examines the brave attempts by major makes such as Kaiser-Frazer, Willys, Packard, Studebaker, Tucker, Nash and Hudson, etc, to compete with the 'Big Three' in America following WWII.

Known as the 'Independents' these automakers were the first to introduce all-new models in an attempt to increase their market share and ensure the future. Following the initial post-war boom, and as that early unique styling became stale, the Big Three introduced fresher designs at cut-throat prices. The resulting fall in sales forced the Independents to downsize, enter niche markets and merge for survival. A horsepower race using V8 engines, which were considered the essential powerplant, also forced the smaller automakers into spending more money developing more powerful engines, eventually abandoning traditional large straight six and straight eight engines.

Innovation by the smaller independent automakers was never an issue, as will be revealed. There were many efforts by American automobile companies to try and fill

small niche markets, including sports cars to capture a piece of the new and exciting post-war, open two-seaters and GT market so dominated by British and European manufacturers. Some of these sports models were designed by the larger Independents, while dozens more backyard enthusiasts or racing-based builders attempted to create the perfect, low volume American sports car.

Some introduced sub-compact and compact models in an attempt to persuade American buyers that small was good. Yet, even the diminutive, microcar-sized King Midget was ultimately doomed in the 'Bigger is Better' American market.

American cars of the 1950s featured matchless innovations and lots of style. It was the jet age, and the American automobile manufacturers incorporated every styling cue they could from aircraft and the emerging

Loads of chrome, jet-like hood ornaments and two-toning were only a few of the many styling cues found on most American cars of the 1950s. (Courtesy Andrew Mort)

space age into their latest car designs. In addition, after more than a decade of the 'Great Depression,' and then war, Americans were looking for a brighter future. Automobiles epitomized this with lots of brilliant chrome and bright or pastel colors in two- and three-tone paint schemes and interiors with lots of brightwork and equally exciting textures and materials.

This TWD book contains detailed captions and supportive text, combined with the use of contemporary brochures, period advertisements, factory photos, and nearly 70 new, unpublished color photos of restored examples, to relate the significance of these historic vehicles. It will look at all the major makers focusing on the innovations, unique styling and features, and why, ultimately, all failed. Where possible, production totals have been included, as have important specifications on

There were literally dozens and dozens of niche American car builders following WWII who hoped to find a market and build a volume car. Many were microcars or small cars, but a substantial number were sports cars inspired by the likes of Jaguar, Ferrari, MG, Allard, Healey, and others. (1954 Cunningham C-3 Vignale pictured.) (Courtesy Hyman Motors Ltd)

Space age styling and wild design studies were also characteristic of the 1950s. Some of these ideas would eventually find their way into production cars. Then again, the four-seater 1958 Studebaker-Packard Astral dream car, powered by atomic energy and capable of running on one or no wheels, wasn't one of them. (Author's collection)

particular models. Production totals were calculated by both calendar and model year, and, in many cases both these numbers varied considerably from source to source and should not be considered as one hundred per cent accurate.

It should also be noted that Studebaker was one independent with a long history in building trucks. The styling of its larger trucks was adapted directly from its smaller pickup truck models. Hudson also built pickup trucks and for a brief time only (1946-47) following WWII. (Author's collection)

STUDEBAKER TRANSTAR

1 to 2 ton heavy-duty
9,000 to 24,000 lbs. g.v.w.
29,000 to 42,000 lbs. g.c.w.

TRUCKS DO MORE COST LESS!!!

BEER
HEY COUSIN!
BUY A DOZEN

Kaiser-Frazer

Following WWII, industrialist Henry J Kaiser joined Graham-Paige executive Joseph Frazer and formed a new car company to compete head-on with the well-established automakers. Whereas Joe Frazer had a rich automotive background, Kaiser was an industrialist who had developed a nation-wide reputation for getting things done, and done well.

Based in Willow Run in the former bomber plant, the two hired famed designer Howard 'Dutch' Darrin to create the styling of the all-new Kaiser and Frazer (K-F)

This pre-production brochure describes the originally proposed FWD Kaiser which featured 'Packaged Power.' After just two prototypes were built, engineering problems and costs resulted in adopting a traditional drivetrain powered by a 115hp, 226.2cu.in (3.7L), L-head 'Continental' Six. Continental had supplied engines to many American manufacturers over the years before becoming part of the Kaiser empire. (Author's collection)

This Frazer Manhattan model was about $400 more expensive than the Standard version. It featured four bumper guards, broadcloth upholstery, carpeting, a rear armrest, and fancier steering wheel, amongst other things. It is painted in its original two-tone Doeskin (tan) with a Buckeye Maroon roof. (Author's collection)

cars. Darrin's fresh, modern-looking Kaiser and better appointed Frazer models were unveiled early in 1946.

Unfortunately, production delays and the switch from FWD to RWD on the Kaiser car cost the firm time and sales. As of June 1946 K-F had orders for over 650,000 cars, yet just over 156,000 Kaiser and Frazer models were delivered by the end of 1947.

Novel in design, these cars were powered by the well-proven Continental Six engine that had become part of Kaiser Industries. Sales climbed in 1948 to 181,316 units, but in 1949 production tumbled to 58,281 as the

Forecast of the Future

'Forecast of the Future' was how Kaiser promoted its 1947 'low-price field' sedans. "There are sound functional reasons for those truly modern lines which, flowing in unbroken grace from the headlamps to rear deck, give the Kaiser a surprisingly slender appearance despite the unusual roominess." It was also noted that the seats were 62in wide, and the "... new beauty of line is complemented by many fashionable, harmonizing interior and exterior color schemes." (Author's collection)

Custom Car Beauty

'Custom Car Beauty' was the header for the Frazer brochure description. Despite being virtually identical to the Kaiser, the slightly up-market Frazer possessed "... a slender exterior and a simplicity of line which eliminates unnecessary ornamentation." (Author's collection)

The top-of-the-line Frazer model in 1951 was the Frazer four-door convertible, which featured a fully automatic power top. All Frazers were built on a 123.5in wheelbase. (Author's collection)

The Frazer Vagabond was considered by K-F as the "smart successor to the station wagon." The company boasted that the sedan could be converted into a "spacious carrier" in ten seconds for sports or business use. (Author's collection)

other automakers introduced new post-war models. 1950 was a banner year for the industry and K-F enjoyed an increase in sales to 146,911 cars. Since the post-war boom was already slowing, the fledgling company had introduced unique models, interiors filled with colorful space age materials and numerous new innovative ideas.

Frazer introduced its 1951 models in March 1950, but sales totaled fewer than 11,000 units by the end of the model year, despite extensive facelifts. Alas, it would be the last year these fine cars were offered, with Joe Frazer departing.

The 1951 Kaiser models were completely re-designed and would remain virtually unchanged until its disappearance in 1955. The design was penned once again by Dutch Darrin who created a handsome and distinctive automobile. The unique 'Darrin Dip' was incorporated at the front of the roof, while the overall styling of the new Kaiser was described as 'Anatomic Design.' The term was based on the increased head, shoulder and legroom provided to perfectly suit the anatomy of the human body.

One of the most stylish Frazer models in 1951 was the Frazer Manhattan hardtop, offered "… in two beautiful versions, one covered in lustrous nylon (illustrated) and the other in smart new finishes." (Author's collection)

For 1951 the Kaiser chassis and drivetrain were part of the 'Anatomic Engineering.' Kaiser bragged about its "exclusive spring suspension" that took the shock instead of the occupants, and its 'Truline' steering and lower center of gravity which "… makes the stopping power of the brakes more effective." (Author's collection)

The 1951 Kaiser Special Club Coupe was a base model, but still included 'Anatomic Design.' Anatomic design meant that "… control tower vision, tuck-away tire well, bin opening package compartment …" and other features were exclusive to Kaiser models. (Author's collection)

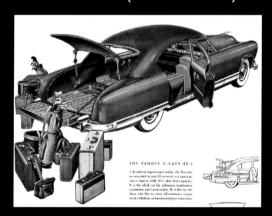

Similar in concept to the Frazer Vagabond, the differently styled 1951 Kaiser Traveler – 2-cars in-1 as it was advertised – came as a two- and four-door sedan. The four-door (pictured) with the backseat folded provided 104cu. ft of space. The wood-ribbed floor and double-hinged rear opening allowed for easy loading. (Author's collection)

K-F announced in 1951 that its Henry J sedan was "the most important new car in America." Henry J Kaiser saw himself as the new Henry Ford who was offering the country the Kaiser version of the Model T. Here was a four-cylinder car which was the lowest priced model in the low price field. An attempt was also made to sell a slightly remodeled, re-badged Henry J as the Sears Allstate (1952-1953) through Sears, Roebuck department stores. The idea flopped, selling only 1566 cars in 1952 and 797 in the first half of '53. (Author's collection)

The two-tone vinyl and cloth interiors found in all the Kaiser models was far more stylish than those seen in its competitors. Wide whitewall tires, twin mirrors, a Continental kit, factory radio, heater and clock, an external sunvisor and seatbelts were all appreciated features that also provided a 'Jet Age' fifties look.

Another move to remain competitive and solvent was through the introduction of the new compact Henry J, announced in September 1950. Surprisingly, the Henry J was not one of Howard 'Dutch' Darrin's projects, although he did make some changes to the American Metal Products of Detroit design. Generally, the Henry J has often been considered one of the cleaner and prettier cars of the 1950s.

1953 *Henry J*

POWERED BY A CHOICE OF
2 GREAT ENGINES

EASIEST TO RUN
EASIEST TO SERVICE
EASIEST TO MAINTAIN

Supersonic 4 America's most famous "Four," now mightier, thriftier than ever. L-head design; bore 3⅛ inches, stroke 4¾ inches; brake horsepower 68 at 4000 r.p.m., compression ratio 7.0 to 1; aluminum alloy pistons; two compression and one oil control ring. Full pressure lubrication. Performance and economy *proved* over millions of miles!

Supersonic 6

Smoother, livelier, thriftier than ever! L-head design; bore 3⅛ inches, stroke 3½ inches; brake horsepower 80 at 3800 r.p.m.; compression ratio 7.0 to 1; aluminum alloy pistons; two compression and one oil control ring. Full pressure lubrication. Up to 30 miles per gallon of gasoline.

The Compact Henry J was available in only one body style, but offered a choice of two engines: the 68hp, four-cylinder L-head, or the 80hp L-head six. These engines were supplied by Willys-Overland. (Author's collection)

The 1953 Kaiser was called the "world's first safety-first car" by K-F. Features included: safer, easier Curve-Master steering; safer oversized brakes; a safer lighting system; Neva-Lok wraparound bumpers; safety door locks; a one-piece safety-mounted windscreen designed to pop-out on impact; a safety padded dash; recessed instruments; extra foot room for a safer seating position; and a safety-angle seat that balanced you more safely. (Author's collection)

You ride in beauty, as well as safety . . . surrounded . . . as seen here in the '53 Kaiser Manhattan—by richest cushion-textured Luxura fabrics, styled and loomed expressly for Kaiser . . . set off by glamorous new deep-embossed Bambu Vinyl and Boucle Vinyl, all tastefully keyed to a harmonious symphony of color.

As well as being promoted as safer, a Kaiser interior was well ahead of its time in design, colors and textiles. Yet, despite all the benefits of buying a Kaiser, production fell to around 30,000 units, and, in October 1953, a net loss of nearly $11 million was reported. (Author's collection)

Available only as a two-door, buyers had a choice of either an economical four-cylinder engine Corsair or the more powerful Corsair DeLuxe Six. The former was proclaimed to be the lowest-priced, full-sized American sedan.

By the end of February changes were already unveiled for 1952, with new front and rear end styling, improved steering, better cold weather starting and a 4.27 to 1 rear axle for even greater fuel economy.

Kaiser was also now seeking another car line to replace the Frazer and that was solved by the purchase of Willys-Overland (see Willys).

For 1953 the larger Kaiser line saw some model choices dropped and minor changes made in trim and specifications only. A more major facelift took place in 1954, but sales continued to decline falling below 10,000 units.

Only the Kaiser Manhattan model was offered in

"Get on Easiest Street" was the slogan for the 1953 Henry J. K-F pointed out 39 finer ways to keep you on "Easiest Street" for years, like the option of a rear seat that folded flat to provide 58cu.ft of cargo deck on Vagabond and Traveler models. (Author's collection)

1955. Of the 1231 sedans built, 1021 were shipped to Argentina. The tooling, etc, was then sent to Argentina and became part of IKA (Industrias Kaiser Argentina). Known there as the Kaiser Carabela, these sedans would be built from 1958-1962. Of the almost 575,000 Kaiser, Frazer and Willys cars built in America an estimated 500,000 were Kaisers.

The Kaiser styling by Darrin was unique in many ways. Its tall greenhouse was designed to accommodate the wearing of hats, while the eyebrow-style windscreen provided better all-round vision. This is a Manhattan, whereas the top-of-the-line Dragon featured a padded 'Bambu' vinyl roof, 14-carat gold fender script, optional chrome wire wheels, standard wide whitewall tires, and a quieter, ultra-luxurious interior. (Author's collection)

The Kaiser Darrin sports car bore most of the traditional styling cues its cars were known for, and, like the sedans, always incorporated unique design features. Apart from the rather obvious front end styling, the Darrin featured distinctive doors that slid into the front fenders to provide access to the interior. When Kaiser production ended (435 cars built), Darrin took control of the production of the car to become an independent manufacturer (100 built). (Author's collection)

Studebaker-Packard
Packard

Packard, Pierce-Arrow and Peerless – or the 3Ps as they were known in the first three decades of the twentieth century – were the top American luxury car builders.

The Packard brothers had a successful manufacturing company producing incandescent lamps and transformers, but when James Ward Packard encountered numerous problems with his 1898 Winton, the brothers turned their attention to building an automobile in 1899.

By 1901 the famous Packard slogan 'Ask the man who owns one' had been coined. In 1902 the

In 1945 Packard was America's oldest independent surviving automaker, yet it was soon to discover a very different marketplace. Following the war, many of the company's independent suppliers no longer existed and securing steel was difficult. Inefficient assembly procedures, strikes and shortages, coupled with government price restrictions, thwarted the company resuming production. These labor problems and material shortages resulted in a low production run of only 30,793 1946 models. (Courtesy Andrew Mort)

Ohio Automobile Company, which had been handling production, officially became the Packard Motor Car Company.

Competition successes resulted in a reputation for quality, which, in turn, led to a steady increase in sales.

In a valiant attempt to remain one of the premiere manufacturers of luxury cars during the great depression, Packard introduced a six-cylinder car in 1937 to broaden its market share. Although Packard sales skyrocketed to 109,518 units, 90 per cent of production were lower-priced models. This helped Packard stave-off bankruptcy, but severely damaged its reputation as a builder of prestige cars.

By 1941 Packard was already building Rolls-Royce Merlin aircraft engines for military use, as well as other Defense Department production which made the company money, but hindered car production and sales levels fell. Then Packard committed what many feel was a blunder by selling the dies of its prestige Junior and Senior cars to Russia, leaving it with only the newly released Clipper model. In peacetime, Russia would produce Packard-like ZIMs and ZILs.

Packard was quick to resume car production in October 1945 with its Clipper models. Pent-up demand for new cars had created an opportunity for Packard to increase its market percentage. The Clipper styling still looked newer than most of the competition, despite the fact it was virtually identical to the pre-war model.

The 1946 Packard Clipper was initially offered as a four-door sedan only, but by April that year a two-door sedan joined the line-up, along with a full range of cars on either a 120in or a 127in wheelbase. Still, further delays meant the 147in 7-passenger models weren't available until August.

Packard announced there would be no changes in

Brand-new for '46 — and, more than ever before, it's

AMERICA'S No.1 GLAMOUR CAR!

The 1946 Packard Clipper would eventually be built in many guises. This example of "America's No. 1 Glamour Car," as it was advertised, is a Deluxe Clipper Eight four-door sedan. Due to production problems, Packard noted in its advertisements, "So, if you have to wait a little while for your new 1946 Packard Clipper, we hope you'll be patient. Here is a car worth waiting for, if ever there was one!" (Author's collection)

Never before in Packard's history has there been an announcement ad like this!

Packard ads proudly stated in 1947 that, "By continuing to build this superlatively fine motor car over into 1947, we do not have to stop production to 'tool up' for changes." In reality, production was now in full swing and Packard was hoping to make up for lost time and sales. Production of 1947 models (1948s were introduced earlier in September) was a meager 35,836 units, dropping the one-time leader of the independent automakers to fifth place in sales, and a loss of almost $5 million. (1947 Custom Super Club Sedan shown.) (Author's collection)

its 1947 models. Supplier strikes and further government involvement in steel allocation hindered production throughout the industry, but more so in Packard's old, out-dated Detroit plants.

For 1948 the first new post-war Packard was unveiled, led by a stylish convertible. More slab-sided with round bathtub styling, as was the styling trend, calendar sales rose to 98,897 cars – an increase of 88 per cent. A total of seventeen body styles were offered

'Stately styling' best describes this 1948 Packard Custom Eight with its traditional-shaped Packard grille. The egg-crate insert, formal roofline, restrained use of chrome, and wide whitewall tires were unique to the Custom line. The fresh styling won Packard many design awards. All Packards, except taxicab models, were powered by eight-cylinder engines. (Courtesy Ron Dancey)

Packard interiors were always luxurious, finely appointed, and pleasing to the eye with excellent ergonomics. Unlike many American cars of this era, the dashboard had a clean, uncluttered look thanks to the use of mostly push-button controls. (Courtesy Ron Dancey)

The Custom Eight was powered by the 160hp version of the 365cu.in (6.0L) straight eight, featuring nine main bearings, hydraulic valve lifters and a Carter two-barrel carburetor. (Courtesy Ron Dancey)

on four different wheelbases ranging from 120in to 141in with a choice of three eight-cylinder models.

Established in 1899, the 1949 models were heralded as the 'Golden Anniversary' Packards, but there were no new models and no changes in styling. The biggest news was the new 2-speed 'Ultramatic' transmission. Despite the lack of change and simple model redefinition, calendar sales rose in 1949 to a post-war record of 104,593 vehicles.

Again the 1949 'Golden Anniversary'

THE EIGHT • 130 HP   THE SUPER EIGHT • 145 HP   THE CUSTOM EIGHT • 160 HP

Despite the fact the classic MGM film and L Frank Baum book *The Wizard of Oz* had debuted in 1939, star Judy Garland was more popular than ever and still belting out tunes from that classic movie. Thus, Packard's play on words was immediately recognizable when describing the 1948 Packard convertible. The ad copy began, "Watch the envious glances – hear the enthusiastic 'Oh's!' and 'Ah's!' – when this sleek, glossy Packard convertible glides up to the curb!" The convertible was offered with the 145hp Super or the 160hp Custom straight eight engine. (Author's collection)

Designed by the Wizards of "Ah's!"

The 1948 Packard line-up consisted of three eight-cylinder models. Packard described its straight eight engines for 1948 as being "free-breathing gas misers." Ads boasted that, "They're delighting Packard owners with up to 10% more miles per gallon!" (Author's collection)

New Golden Anniversary Packard *Custom*, shown at left, is more than ever *America's most luxurious motor car.* Two stunning new body creations, both powered by the famed 160-horsepower Packard Custom Eight engine.

ASK THE MAN WHO OWNS ONE

In 1949, Packard stressed its fifty-year heritage as America's oldest independent surviving automobile builder, as there were few changes to its model range to promote. In fact, leftover 1948 models (30,095 cars) were issued with new serial numbers and designated as anniversary Packards. Changes included an increase in horsepower throughout the range, and the Super Eights became longer wheelbase models. (Author's collection)

Packard models were re-designated as 1950 models on October 1st 1949. All that was new were additional options, particularly those first seen on the Custom line that were now offered on all models. Packard's much hailed automatic transmission was now available throughout the line-up.

Due to supplier strikes, a strike at the Packard plant, and little change in the line-up from 1949, sales slumped and a mere 31,959 designated 1950 Packard models

There were nine reasons to buy a 1950 Packard, but the most important reason was the company's new 'Ultramatic' transmission. It was stressed that Packard's automatic transmission was, "... superior to all other automatic drives." Despite all this hoopla, sales fell by more than 60 per cent and Packard lost $700,000. (Author's collection)

Great hopes were pinned on the first all-new Packard in a decade, designed to compete head-on with Cadillac and other higher end GM models, as well as Lincoln. The base 1951 Model 200, in the 24th Series, was priced to vie for high-end Buick customers, while the Patrician 300 (pictured) and 400 that had replaced the Super and Custom Eights, were aimed at Cadillac. Interior, power output, and trim differentiated each model. (Author's collection)

were built. With sales declining by over 60 per cent Packard lost $700,000 in 1950.

In 1951 Packard finally introduced its first all-new model range, which included the 200, 250, 300 and Patrician 400. These were all differentiated in trim with only the 200 being offered on a shorter 122in wheelbase. The new Packards were longer, wider and lower and featured the new 'Horizon Vision' curved windscreens, and full-length front fenders that blended into slightly bulging rear fenders. For 1951 the 'Clipper' nameplate was dropped and production increased to 69,921 vehicles.

Although annual model changes were announced, starting in 1951, there were only minor changes in appearance for '52, yet model production jumped to 81,341 cars.

For 1953 the changes in models and styling was only slightly more dramatic. The Clipper name reappeared as a base model and the Cavalier basically

In 1952 the Packard Pan American show car was unveiled. It won the coveted top honours at the International Motor Sports Show in New York as the car with the most outstanding design and engineering achievement. Up to six more were thought to have been built (hearses, flower cars, ambulances, etc) by professional car builder, Henney Company of Freeport, Illinois. Henney had traditionally been responsible for many of Packard's post-war limousines. This stylish convertible met with rave reviews and was the direct inspiration for the Packard Caribbean that appeared late in 1953. (Author's collection)

The New Packard **CLIPPER**
Big-Car Value At Medium-Car Cost!

Now Packard offers an entirely new line in a wide range of advanced contour-styled models —the new *Packard CLIPPERS*—for big-car value at *medium-car cost*. These true products of Packard experience, engineering and skill give you *real Packard quality*, inside and out, for just a few hundred dollars more than cars in the *low-priced* field.

Powered by Packard's mighty Thunderbolt Eight Engines, they are the roomiest cars in their price class—with seats as wide as these cars are high and with the largest luggage compartment of any sedan. So no matter what you may plan to spend for a car, PACKARD—with *two* great new lines for '53—offers you your *best motorcar investment*.

For 1953 the Clipper name re-appeared as a base model or Junior line, while the Cavalier essentially replaced the 300 range with the addition of the Caribbean convertible joining the Mayfair hardtop. Model sales rose to 90,268 vehicles, but the profit margin was decreasing. (Author's collection)

(Below) The Mayfair two-door hardtop had been unveiled in 1952 as a response to America's newly discovered fondness for sportier looking cars that resembled a convertible, but had the comfort and convenience of a two-door sedan. The 1953 Mayfair was changed only slightly. (Courtesy Andrew Mort)

The 1953 Mayfair found 5150 owners willing to pay a base price of $3280. It was Packard's only hardtop, and borrowed the Clipper DeLuxe side trim and the rear fender 'jet pods' first seen on the top-of-the-line 1951 Patrician 400. The 'fishtail' rear end look was also shared with other models. (Courtesy Andrew Mort)

replaced the 300 range, with additional nameplates added including the Mayfair hardtop. Yet, the big news was the Caribbean Convertible which was actually built by the Mitchell-Bentley Company of Ionia, Michigan which had been contracted by Packard to convert 750 standard Packard convertibles. Surprisingly, 1953 model year production of the only slightly changed line-up still topped 90,000 units, yet 63,874 of those cars were the lower priced Clipper models.

The 1954 Packard models were not unveiled until January 1954 due to the purchase of the Briggs Manufacturing Company by Chrysler in 1953; Packard bodies had been built by Briggs since 1940. Although Packard responded quickly by establishing its own body building facility it wasn't able to introduce the all-new models it had hoped.

The 1954 models received minor facelifts, trim

The 1953 Mayfair featured an up-scale vinyl and leather interior with chrome roof bows accentuating its all-vinyl headliner. The base price of Packard's only hardtop in 1953 was a reasonable $3280, yet sales totaled only 5150 units. (Courtesy Andrew Mort)

The 1953 Mayfair hardtop was powered by the Packard inline, five-bearing, L-head 327cu.in (5.4L) straight eight rated at 180bhp. (Courtesy Andrew Mort)

Two hardtops were offered in 1954, known as the Pacific and the Panama. The Clipper was now being promoted as a separate model line, thus the hardtop models were referred to as the Clipper Panama (165hp) and the Packard Pacific (212hp). (Author's collection)

changes and a new Clipper model, along with a host of name changes in this short model run which netted a mere 30,965 sales.

1954 is also remembered as the pivotal year, where the company made a bad situation even worse. This was the year Packard lost its jet engine and marine diesel contracts. Money was spent re-engineering a straight eight engine that was replaced the following year by the new line of V8s, but the decision to buy failing Studebaker was the beginning of the end.

Packard had seen the other Independents merge and now Packard was left with Studebaker as the only alternative. Although renamed the Studebaker-Packard Corporation it was Packard that bought Studebaker.

Studebaker did have more modern production facilities and built cars that better suited the quickly

Only 750 Packard Caribbeans were built before the 1954 models were introduced. The Caribbean convertible was the most expensive Packard in the line-up, with a list price of $6100. Standard equipment included: power steering; power brakes; power windows; a power seat; dual heaters and defrosters; a full, rich leather interior; a three-way radio with power antenna; a continental spare tire; and five classic Kelsey-Hayes chrome wire wheels. The 1954 Packard Caribbean convertible rode on a 122in wheelbase and was powered by a 212hp, 359cu.in (5.9L), L-head inline eight-cylinder engine with 9-main bearings and a Carter 4-bbl carb. (Author's collection)

The 1955 Clipper Custom Four-Door was nearly 18ft long and powered by Packard's new 245hp V8. The base Clipper V8 engine was rated at 225hp. Note the Clipper no longer carried the Packard crest, but rather bore a sailing ship's wheel as an emblem. The Clipper received only fresh front and rear styling. (Author's collection)

The 1955 Packard 'Four Hundred' hardtop was a handsome car, most often in a two-tone paint scheme, but the '55 line-up was dubbed the 'Reynolds Wrap' model due to the wide band of trim that encircled the body. The Four Hundred was powered by a 260hp, 352cu.in (5.8L) V8. Only 7206 examples were sold. (Author's collection)

changing marketplace where power, performance, youth and medium- or low-priced models were the most popular and fastest growing automotive segments, but the site in South Bend, Indiana was a losing concern.

For 1954 the Packard Caribbean Convertible was even more luxurious than the original '53 version. Features included: the newly-styled headlamp rims; chrome trim on its hood scoop and lower rear wheel cut-outs; stylish two-tone paintwork color-keyed to the interior; Caribbean script on the front fenders; and side molding that swept off the rear cowl and slipped below the crest of the rear fenders into distinctive integrated taillights.

In 1955 an all-new Packard senior line was introduced. Powered by a line of four new V8 engines,

the cars featured an innovative torsion bar suspension, a greatly improved automatic transmission, and sported slimmer, fresh, crisp styling. Sales rose to 55,247 vehicles when the model year concluded early in August, but problems with its new automatic transmission and the build quality at the hastily organized Conner Avenue body plant resulted in a lot of negative press.

Packard set its sights on a big year in 1956, but a strike delayed production until October 29th and ultimately only 28,835 cars were built.

Dealers were abandoning Packard at an alarming rate. In 1954 Packard had approximately 2200 franchise outlets, but by the spring of 1956 that number had shrunk to just 1500 nationwide dealers.

In 1955, Packard's top-of-the-line model was again the Caribbean convertible, priced at $5932. With its totally new styling, it was one of just three Senior Packards offered, yet only its side trim was now exclusive to the Caribbean. The last Packard Caribbeans were built in 1956, and a hardtop version joined the convertible. (Courtesy Ron Dancey)

PACKARD CLIPPER, *Supercharged for '57*

Behold the Incomparable

PACKARD

America's only fine car with...

Torsion-Level Ride—the new suspension principle that outmodes coil and leaf springs

Up to 310 Horsepower—giving you mightier wheel-driving force than any other car

Electronic Touch-Button Drive—the only electronically operated finger-touch control

Twin-Traction Safety Differential—for dramatically safer road-grip the year round

The fastest increase in resale value of any car—up as much as 9.6% in the past year

ASK THE MAN WHO OWNS *the New* ONE

PACKARD DIVISION – STUDEBAKER-PACKARD CORPORATION Where Pride of Workmanship *Still* Comes First

In the last Packard Caribbean models the power was increased to 310hp. At this point the hardtop was just a Packard 400 with all the Caribbean luxury add-ons and exclusive side trim. (Author's collection)

(Left) For 1957 Packard offered a McCulloch supercharged Clipper fitted with a Flight-O-matic transmission. At 3000rpm the supercharger would boost power. The Clipper was a bit more than just a Studebaker President with Packard badges and different trim. Also unique to the Packard were rear fins, a different grille and rear end treatment. (Author's collection)

Although Packard had originally bought Studebaker in 1954, attempts were made to merge with American Motors, but it was Curtiss-Wright (C-W) that gained management control in 1956. The move was more of a tax write-off and, as official importer for various makes of German cars, including Mercedes-Benz, a way of acquiring a sales network. C-W also raided what remained of Packard's profitable military contracts and basically left the troubled car business to fend on its own.

In a cost-cutting move, the Detroit Packard plant was closed, as was the year old engine plant. Production was moved to the larger capacity, yet more expensive to operate, Studebaker South Bend facility. The plant could not build the full-size Packards on its assembly lines, which were designed to build mid-size and compact cars. Thus, only two Packards would be badge-engineered Studebaker models starting in 1957, of which only 4809 were built. Yet, for 1957 Packard offered a supercharged Clipper fitted with a Flight-O-matic transmission.

In its final year of production the Packard line-up was expanded to include a hardtop and the sport coupe known

Packard's last hurrah was the ungainly-looking, 120.5in Packard Hawk with its padded armrests and fiberglass front and rear end add-ons. Powered by a 275hp V8, the leather interior featured a front split-benchseat for three. (Author's collection)

From the Home of the Golden Hawks . . .

Packard Hawk

the Finest Tradition of Packard Craftsmanship
a Distinctive New, Full-Powered Sports-Styled Car

The newest member of a long line of distinguished motor cars . . . the power-equipped 1958 Packard Hawk combines for the first time famous Packard luxury and efficiency with dashing sports car styling. All the comfort and quality features that consumers have long associated with Packard automobiles are here . . . plus striking sports car design from the Continent with such exclusive new features as luxurious all-leather seats, weatherproof outside vinyl arm-rests, low slung European frontal styling. A sport-type simulated tire cover completes the picture of motion in action. And talk about performance! The all-new Packard Hawk is powered by a 275 horsepower V-8 engine . . . teamed with a self-lubricating, noiseless Jet-Stream Supercharger that provides quicksilver accelera-tion for unbeatable passing ability at highway cruising speeds. Yes, it's all here in one completely unique and authentic American sports car . . . superior roadability . . . prestige luxury . . . power brakes . . . ample seating room for an entire family. But above all, when you take the wheel of your new Packard Hawk, you can be certain you have made a sound investment in quality—the same quality that has proven itself through the years with satisfied Packard customers the world over.

That wonderful feel of real leather, the gleam of hand-polished surfaces, the array of sports car instruments . . . these are features you note and admire instantly when you see the Packard Hawk. Front seat is wide for three; the rear seat has a fold-away center arm rest for the comfort of both passengers. It is a luxurious interior of functional design, as befits a leading car of the Packard line.

as the Packard Hawk, however, including the wagon and sedan, a total of only 2622 'Packabakers' (as they were rudely referred to) were built. The Packard nameplate would officially be dropped in 1962.

The Pelican, in its many guises as a symbol of the Packard Motor Company, flew for the last time in 1958. (Andrew Mort)

The Predictor was the last Packard show car ever built, and first appeared at the 1956 Chicago Auto Show. Designed by Dick Teague, it was constructed by Ghia in Italy. It was filled with innovations. As the promotion brochure noted, "When you open the Predictor's doors, sliding roof panels over the doors automatically and silently roll back for easy exit and entrance. The roof panels can also be opened for ventilation while the doors remain closed." Other novelties at the time included: swivel seats; a fully retractable rear window; four hidden headlamps (a pair each for city driving and country driving); rear jet pods housing back-up lights and four exhaust ports; push-button transmission; a power trunk lid; a roof-mounted control panel; a wrap-over windshield; and more. (Author's collection)

Studebaker

Henry and Clem Studebaker opened a blacksmith and wagon shop in South Bend, Indiana in 1852 and built horse-drawn vehicles until 1919. Studebaker had begun building bodies for electric car companies in 1897 and then its own electric vehicles (1902-1912), while also building gas-powered cars under the Studebaker-Garford name. Studebaker eventually bought EMF (Everitt-Metzger-Flanders) in 1911 to officially enter into the automobile business.

The company survived the depression and a mildly re-styled Champion Skyway appeared in December 1945, netting Studebaker a quick 19,275 sales.

In May 1946, stylist Raymond Loewy, along with Bob Bourke and Virgil Exner, pushed Studebaker into the limelight with a dramatic new 1947 line-up. It was one of America's first all-new cars. Fresh styling with jet and rocket inspiration, the new Studebakers were expected to take the market by storm. The Studebaker Commander and Champion models were nothing like anyone had ever seen before, especially when it came to the wraparound rear windows on the coupes. Yet, the controversial ultra-modern styling often ended-up drawing as much criticism as it did admiration.

For 1948 only minor facelift changes were made, which included a slightly wider, less cluttered grille, larger parking lights and some added trim. Model year sales rose to 164,753 units, which was slightly less than Kaiser-Frazer, but good for 9th overall in the industry. Market share had risen from Studebaker's traditional three per cent to nearly five.

For 1949 there were only minor changes, but that was the year the Big Three introduced their first all-new line-ups, not to mention competing with a new Nash and only one-year old step-down Hudson. Still, calendar sales

increased to 228,000 cars and placed Studebaker eighth in the industry, ahead of the face-lifted Kaiser-Frazer models, but model year sales slid to just 129,303 cars.

1947 saw one of America's first all-new cars. The Studebaker Commander and Champion models were nothing like previous models and, in fact, nothing like anyone had ever seen before when it came to the wraparound rear windows on the coupes. (Courtesy Norm McWaters)

Studebaker ad copy noted, "They're more than fresh 1948 interpretations of the 'new look' in cars that's a Studebaker style mark. They're a dramatic encore to over a year and a half of the most sensational new-car success in motoring." The 1948 convertible model had debuted in '47 and was the first open Studebaker since 1938, with close to 18,000 sold. (Author's collection)

Described as, "… a new vision of loveliness inside and out," the 1949 Studebakers again featured a new grille, along with winged badges. A new long wheelbase Land Cruiser featured nylon upholstery as part of the 'glory in new luxury' and 'new vogue' interiors by Studebaker stylists. Note the full wraparound rear window on the Champion Starlight coupe. (Author's collection)

For 1950 Raymond Loewy introduced a dramatic restyling of the line-up. In retrospect, even Loewy didn't like the 'bullet' or 'spinner' nose when adapted to a much taller, higher sitting automobile. Still, production spun upwards reaching 344,164 sales in this high tide year for the industry.

With the introduction of the Studebaker V8 in 1951 optimism was high, but the market had peaked and sales slipped to 268,559 cars.

Mildly face-lifted, the following year saw sales

tumble again to just 186,219 units. A new Studebaker was needed.

When the all-new Raymond Lowey coupes were unveiled in 1953 it caused such a sensation that even Studebaker was caught off-guard. Studebaker had planned two-thirds production of four-door sedans and one-third coupes. The demand was the reverse and Studebaker was never able to produce enough coupes.

For 1954 the styling changes were minimal, but the Conestoga station wagon was added. Sales fell again to 169,899 cars, as did profits.

In 1954 Studebaker and Packard joined together in order to survive. Perhaps it was an omen when Studebaker sales decreased by over fifty per cent to just

Here it is, America! The "next look" in cars!

In 1950 Studebaker felt it was the 'next look' in cars, but the bullet nose was not universally embraced. Others had a similar look, even Ford, but the American public wasn't really ready to buy it. Mechanically, power was up and there was a new front coil suspension and improved steering. Zero to 60mph (100km/h) times when equipped with the six-cylinder engine were just over 16 seconds. (Author's collection)

Studebaker's 1952 convertible looked very much at home in this upper class setting, but was aimed at the middle class market. (Author's collection)

Historically, throughout the fifties, Studebaker promoted its V8 for economy as well as power. This illustration is from a 1952 promotional book. (Author's collection)

81,930 cars. It was soon discovered Studebaker had not revealed its true break-even point was an annual model production run of 282,000 units, and not 165,000 cars.

For 1955, styling remained basically the same, except for a heavily chromed front end. Sales did increase to 133,826 cars, despite a strike that lasted over a month, but Studebaker-Packard reported a $27.9 million loss.

In 1956 it was Bob Bourke's responsibility to create an all-new look on a shoestring budget. Bourke was equal to the task. The four new models of the 1956 Studebaker Hawks were dramatic in appearance, with their bold grilles, sculpted sides, small fins and two-tone colors. The Sky Hawk was a popular alternative as it was equipped with the 289cu.in Studebaker V8 and came without the fins. Meanwhile, Studebaker-Packard became part of Curtiss-Wright.

Studebakers followed the industry trend in rear end styling for 1957. The new fins would continue to grow in size in 1958 and '59.

The new Studebakers were not a smashing success and sales slumped to 74,738 cars, with 1958 being even worse, totaling just 53,830 units.

Yet, Harold Churchill had a plan and that was to have Studebaker compete in markets ignored by the Big Three. He was the man behind (continued on page 44)

Again in 1953, with the beautifully sculpted and executed 1953 Starliner designed by Raymond Loewy and Robert Bourke, Studebaker proved that superb styling didn't always sell cars. The base Studebaker Coupes were powered by an 85hp, 169.6cu.in (2.8L), L-head six-cylinder, with a live rear axle, semi-elliptic leaf springs and four-wheel hydraulic brakes riding on a 120.5in wheelbase. The 1954 Studebaker Commander Regal was a spin-off of the Sunliner line. (Author's collection)

Studebaker went for a fully chromed front end for 1955, which was considered rather garish, even for the 1950s. It re-styled the front end in 1956. Wheelbase for the sedan was 116.5in. (Courtesy Andrew Mort)

Simple elegance best describes the look of the interior for this 1955 Studebaker Commander. While a basic six-cylinder sedan was priced at $1783, the top-of-the-line 259cu.in (4.2L) V8 cost $2381. (Courtesy Andrew Mort)

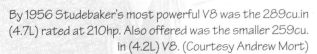

By 1956 Studebaker's most powerful V8 was the 289cu.in (4.7L) rated at 210hp. Also offered was the smaller 259cu.in (4.2L) V8. (Courtesy Andrew Mort)

Two-toning was all the rage in 1955, as seen on this Commander four-door sedan. A two- or three-tone paint scheme provided even the basic sedan with a lot of added pizzazz for little money. (Courtesy Andrew Mort.)

Although re-styled, a bold, heavily chromed, front end was again characteristic of the 1956 Studebaker sedans and wagons. Of the 133,827 cars Studebaker produced in 1956 only 11,685 station wagons were built. (Courtesy Andrew Mort)

Studebaker also offered its all-steel station wagon in 1956. This 2-door Pinehurst wagon was powered by a 4-barrel, 289cu.in (4.7L) V8 and loaded with optional equipment, such as power steering, air-conditioning, a radio, deluxe steering wheel, full wheel discs and whitewall tires. (Courtesy Andrew Mort)

Studebaker followed the industry trend in rear end styling for 1957 when it grew fins, although these fins would continue to grow in size in 1958 and '59. (Author's collection)

From the Home of
the Golden Hawks...

Studebaker *Scotsman 4-Door Sedan*

Full Size...Full Power...Maximum Economy

Enjoy complete comfort for six persons in this new Scotsman 4-door sedan . . . the quick response of the Sweepstakes Six L-head engine of 101 horsepower . . . up to 29 miles per gallon operating economy . . . and the lowest initial cost and depreciation of all major makes of cars. You'll like the smart, functional design of this new Studebaker Scotsman . . . the new Flightstream roofline of 1958 . . . and styling that will stay up-to-date for more than just one year. You're sure to see the long term value in the attractive, functional interiors—built to stand hard family use. And you'll especially appreciate the many equipment features which are all included in the low initial price. For driving cross-town or cross-country, you'll find this new full-sized Scotsman your most satisfactory, most economical purchase. And mile after mile you continue to benefit from the bonus built into all Studebaker products—*extra craftsmanship* that assures low up-keep and dependable operation.

The most economical, easiest-to-service powerplant on the market!

Studebaker's dependable, 7.8 to 1 compression, Sweepstakes Six . . . standard in the Scotsman models, has many advanced features. Water jackets that run the full length of the cylinder walls . . . full pressure lubrication . . . four automatic controls . . . moisture-proof ignition . . . 12-volt electrical system . . . a Celeron timing gear that runs quietly, never needs adjustment. It's America's most dependable Six.

It's hard to believe in today's politically correct times that in 1958 Studebaker would promote its cheapest model as the Studebaker Scotsman. Powered by an 'economical' 101hp, six-cylinder L-head engine, known as the 'Sweepstakes Six,' this model was available in such colors as Glasgow Gray, Glen Green, Loch Blue, Midnight Black, and Parchment White.

the compact Lark which resulted in sales spiraling to over 130,000 units in both 1959 and 1960.

In the 1960s, despite the introduction of the fast, stylish Avanti and continued interest in the Lark and Hawk models, sales fell, due in large part to the closing of South Bend. It was no secret, though, that Studebaker was attempting to bring vehicle production to an end, and this was the just another step along that road to forming what would ultimately be the Studebaker-Worthington Corporation. All production was transferred to the Studebaker assembly plant in Hamilton, Ontario in March 1964, and it all came to an end after 114 years of wagon and vehicle production when the Hamilton factory was closed in 1966.

The Lark caused a sensation when introduced by Studebaker in 1959, but some of it was at dealer level only. No longer did Studebaker offer a full-size sedan. The line-up was now a choice between the compact Lark and the sporty Silver Hawk. Brisk initial sales of the stylish Lark helped quell dealer concern, although Studebaker-Packard was no longer competing with just the Big Three, plus AMC, but the import market, too. (Author's collection)

The Studebaker Champ was the firm's entry in the lucrative pickup truck market in NA. It was available as a half ton or three-quarter ton with four engine and four transmission choices. (Author's collection)

Hudson-Nash

Hudson

The Hudson Motor Company was established in 1909 by Roy D Chapman from funds provided by department store magnate J L Hudson. The firm soon built a fine reputation for reliability and performance, while being a pioneer in the field of closed cars in the 1920s. During the depression, the firm remained solvent, but struggled throughout. As the depression ended, sales improved.

Despite parts and materials shortages, strikes, and the time involved in converting to peacetime production, Hudson was one of the few American automobile manufacturers to record a production increase compared to 1941, with 93,870 vehicles built in the 1946 model year.

The high demand for new cars continued into 1947, and Hudson responded by building 103,310 new vehicles. The design changes had been minor as Hudson was about to introduce its first all-new model in almost a decade.

Frank Spring had designed cars and airplanes since the 1920s, before joining the Hudson styling department in 1931. His 'Step-Down' concept conceived in 1941 was ultimately responsible for Hudson's revolutionary production design, which lowered the floor to just 8in off the ground. This also provided a lower centre of gravity for better overall handling and an improvement in ground effects.

The revolutionary 'Step-Down' design would ultimately be copied throughout the industry in the years to come. Meanwhile, the improvement in aerodynamics, combined with Hudson's powerful and reliable straight six engines, resulted in the domination of American stock car racing, which, in turn, sparked a horsepower race that would last for nearly two decades.

Despite the innovation, like the other Independents by the early 1950s, Hudson was fighting for its life.

The Hudson Hornet Club Coupe cost $2742 and was the most popular Hudson model of 1952, yet, despite its stock car racing domination, only 35,921 were built.

1946 Hudson models differed considerably from the pre-war designs, especially when it came to the newly-styled front grille, which was now a die-cast rather than a stamping. The design by Frank Spring and Art Kibiger was also the first to feature a black painted background behind the bars. Not only did this visually give the grille more depth, but it allowed things like the horn, wiring, etc to be painted black and be fitted behind the grille relatively unnoticed. Other exterior changes included: concealed running boards; a new wider beltline; hood ornament; wraparound bumpers; and a two-tone paint option with the darkest color on top rather than below. There were more engine choices and significant interior improvements as well. (Author's collection)

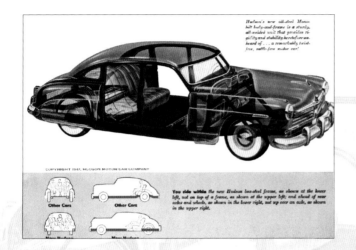

Hudson was another independent quick off the mark, with its all-new post-war design introduced in November 1947. These Hudson models soon became known as the 'Step Down' models due to the all-steel 'Monobilt body and frame' that you stepped down into when entering, rather than stepping up. "And, for even softer going, you also ride not only between the axles, but completely ahead of the rear wheels." (Author's collection)

By 1953 talks of mergers for survival amongst the Independents had begun. Hudson's venture into the compact market with the Jet had not been the expected huge success. Losses mounted, and sales tumbled for the calendar year to just 51,314 cars; only two-thirds what it had been in 1952. In January 1954, Hudson joined Nash in a consolidation to form American Motors.

For 1948 the all-new Hudson cars were again offered in two series with no change in model names, although initially only available as four-door sedans. A Brougham and Club Coupe version became available by year end, and before the '49 models were released a Brougham Convertible joined the line-up. The Super Six and Commodore Six were powered by Hudson's new L-head six-cylinder engine. With a displacement of 262cu.in (4.1L) and rated at 121hp it was the industry's biggest and most powerful six. These six-cylinder models proved to be the most popular. (The Super Eight and Commodore Eight were fitted with the venerable 128hp, 254cu.in [4.2L] straight eight.) Performance was good for the 1950s with 0-40mph (0-60kph) in 12 seconds. Only 117,200 cars were built due to continued labour strife and material shortages. (Author's collection)

In 1949 the Big Three introduced all-new models, which left the Hudson Step Down models looking older. Yet, due to the Monobilt design, the cost of even a mild re-design was still a long way off – 1954, in fact. A 4in shorter wheelbase version of the 119in was introduced in 1950. Hudson also tried to keep pace by upgrading its interiors and changing model names. Sales would peak in 1950 at 145,000 units. (Courtesy Ken Beselaere)

Although not winning in the sales race, Hudson was winning in racing. The Hudson Hornet surprised many with the power of the Twin H-Power six-cylinder engines. Still, the unibody design by Frank Spring also had a lot to do with Tim

Flock easily capturing the 1952 NASCAR Championship. Hornets won 27 of the 34 NASCAR races that season. Of the 48 stock car races in 1952, Hudson Hornet Club Coupes captured 40 checkered flags, living up to its name as the 'unquestioned ruler of the road.' Hudson won the National AAA Stock Car Championship and NASCAR Championship again in 1953. In fact, Hudson was the NASCAR Champion from 1951-1954. (Courtesy Legendary Motorcar)

For 1953 Hudson announced its new compact Jet and Super Jet, powered by a six-cylinder engine rated at 104-114hp with optional aluminum head. The smaller Jet rode on a 105in wheelbase with an overall length of 181in. A two-door version was available only as a Super Jet. It should be noted that famed British racer and car builder Reid Railton, who moved his family to California at the beginning of the war, continued his association with Hudson by becoming a consultant in the late 1940s, and continued in that vein until 1954. (Author's collection)

As this old press photo shows, the 1954 Hudson Italia coupe was a radically different look for Hudson. Powered by a 202cu.in (3.3L) six-cylinder engine, it was based on a Jet chassis created by Hudson Chief Designer Frank Spring and built by Carrozzeria Touring of Milan, and thus a quick name change was made from Super Jet to Italia. Hudson gained international recognition, but in the end only twenty-six of these stylish Italia models were ever produced. (Author's collection)

Nash

Nash Motors Company was established by former GM president Charles Nash in 1916 following the purchase of the Thomas B Jeffrey Company of Kenosha, Wisconsin. Nash prospered and was one of only two American automakers to make a profit in 1932. In 1936,

he hired George Mason of appliance maker Kelvinator Corporation. The two firms merged to form Nash-Kelvinator.

In 1941 Nash was the first American automaker to introduce unibody construction in mass-produced, low-priced cars.

Nash carried over its post-war designs in 1946, and these were continued through until 1949. The 1946 Nash Ambassador was powered by a 112hp, six-cylinder engine. A surprising list of extra charge equipment 'When Available,' included: foam rubber cushions; cruising gear; air-conditioning; a vacuum booster pump; directional signals; an oil bath air cleaner; radio; antenna; and spare tire. (Author's collection)

Following WWII, Nash was the largest, most successful independent automaker. The initial post-war models built were updated 1942 designs.

The first all-new 1949 Nash Ambassador and 600 Airflyte models were clean and simple designs that featured highly creative engineering solutions.

In 1950, the more compact Nash Rambler Airflyte models were added based on styling that was originally

Pictured are two smaller, fully restored Nash Rambler Airflyte models named after the historic Rambler built from 1902-1913 by Thomas B Jeffrey. The blue Nash is a 1950 with rare optional wire wheels and overriders. The turquoise Nash Rambler is a 1951 model. These were well designed compact cars and very spacious considering the 100in wheelbase and relatively short overhangs. The electronically operated, cable-driven convertible top was fully integrated into the body's upper roof structure, which remained fixed for structural rigidity. The partially covered front and rear wheel openings of the envelope body would become a Nash hallmark. (Courtesy Mark Conforzi)

This 1949 Nash was part of the new Airflyte designs that would carry Nash into the next decade. Although only 62in high, the newest Nash also had greater ground clearance than the previous model. Another feature was a one-piece curved windscreen. The Nash was available in two series; the 600 and the higher trim level Ambassador. This 600 model was also capable of achieving over 25mpg.
(Author's collection)

penned during WWII. The actual design was by Nash engineers as the company had no styling department at the time, although it was reportedly inspired by industrial designer Holden Koto.

Nash president George Mason was also involved in every aspect of the car's design and hired sculptor George Petty. Certainly, the Rambler's design was very successful in terms of both packaging and the use of space, with its 100in wheelbase incorporating relatively short overhangs for the era. The compact wheelbase alone was impressive, considering Chrysler and Cadillac built cars with a further 24in between the front and rear wheels. The streamline execution of the partially covered front wheel envelope had now become a Nash hallmark.

The smaller Nash models were a great sales success and made a huge impact on the industry and consumers. While other car manufacturers, such as Kaiser and Willys, experimented with small cars during this period, it was Nash that had the foresight to pursue the development of this market.

By 1951 Nash had continued to expand its line-up, which now consisted of the 121in wheelbase Ambassador; the 112in wheelbase Statesman; and the 100in wheelbase Rambler, all featuring Airflyte styling. (Author's collection)

The 1951 Nash Statesman was a very formal-looking car, yet designed as a six-passenger vehicle with North American families in mind. (Courtesy Andrew Mort)

The Airflyte design at least looked very aerodynamic, particularly when painted in a two-tone combination. Its styling was both dramatic and unique. (Courtesy Andrew Mort)

Despite the formal styling of the '51 Statesman, the seats folded-down for family overnight sleeping. It was a concept the firm introduced to the industry in 1936. Note the factory optional feather mattresses.
(Courtesy Andrew Mort)

For night time ventilation and fresh air while sleeping a set of accessory nylon mesh screen windows was available. These fitted over the window openings and were then tied in place on the inside.
(Courtesy Andrew Mort)

In 1952, Nash advertisements placed the less expensive compact Rambler in very wealthy settings to appeal to a larger market. Just because you were rich didn't mean you couldn't appreciate the 'Continental Flair,' the 'World's safest convertible,' or the Rambler 'all-purpose sedan.' Literary license was clearly evident: the real safety benefits of having fixed window frames on your convertible was never tested; the all-purpose sedan was, in reality, a two-door station wagon; and the Rambler Country Club model pictured was described as a hardtop convertible, when in fact the roof couldn't be removed. (Author's collection)

In 1952 the new Nash models were announced with Pinin Farina styling and production rose to a record 152,141 cars.

Although much touted, the styling was not enough to allow Nash to remain independent. With sales falling below 100,000 units in 1953, negotiations began that would lead to the formation of AMC in 1954 as sales crashed to 67,150 cars.

In 1955, the large Nash models were given extensive facelifts and sales increased to 109,102 cars.

For 1956 the early up-market Nash models were powered by the Packard V8 and fitted with Packard's

For 1954, now in its third year of Pinin Farina styled cars, Nash introduced its next generation of "masterpieces bearing the crest of the man who puts tomorrow on wheels." There were eight new Nash Ambassador and Statesman models. Pictured is the Statesman Super two-door. (Author's collection)

The big news in 1953 was the all-new Nash Rambler model designed again by Pinin Farina and powered by a Flying Scot 85bhp, 184cu.in (3.0L) L-head six-cylinder, or when equipped with the Hydra-Matic transmission, fitted with the 90hp, 195.6cu.in (3.2L) six. (Author's collection)

The short turning radius of the Nash models was seen as one of the many important reasons to buy a Nash in 1955. The big, newly re-styled, long wheelbase Nash turned in a radius of only 6in more than the average of the small, 'low-priced three' (Ford, GM, Chrysler) cars. (Author's collection)

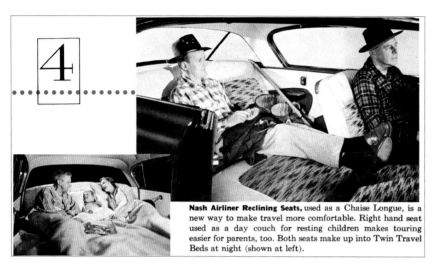

Nash Airliner Reclining Seats, used as a Chaise Longue, is a new way to make travel more comfortable. Right hand seat used as a day couch for resting children makes touring easier for parents, too. Both seats make up into **Twin Travel Beds** at night (shown at left).

Nash continued to offer its sleeping and relaxing option in 1955. The 'Airline reclining seats' could be used as a chaise longue for more comfortable travel. The right-hand seat could be used as a day couch for children, and both seats folded to create 'Twin Travel Beds' at night. Seatbelts were not a promoted option at this time. (Author's collection)

Ultramatic transmission. Later that year, AMC would introduce its own V8 engine. The Statesman and Ambassador were treated to a complete facelift in 1956. The grille, front and rear fenders, hood and taillight treatment were all distinguishing characteristics. The Z-shaped chrome side swipe and outline moldings lent it to the two-toning of the Ambassador body.

In its last year as a marque and model, the Nash Ambassador was powered by AMC's new 255hp, 327cu. in (5.4L) V8 engine. The Ambassador received a major facelift in 1957 which included the first use of quad headlights on any American car, a feature which had just been permitted due to revised highway regulations.

ALL-NEW! Look at that swift sweep of racing line—new Lightning Streak styling. You'll see exciting new colors that make these smart lines even smarter—32 choices in single-tone, two-tone and three-tone.

1957 would be the last year for the Nash nameplate. Nash was still claiming its models were the 'world's finest travel car.' This assertion was based on its 4-beam headlamp system; flow-through dual mufflers to reduce engine back pressure to a minimum; the widest front seat available in the industry; and excellent head and foot room. There was no mention of the new 'Lightning Streak' styling aiding travel, but the Z-shaped chrome side swipe and outline moldings lent themselves to the two-toning of the Ambassador body. (Author's collection)

Nash also entered the sports car market with its Pinin Farina Nash-Healeys. In 1949, Nash president George Mason met Donald Healey. Healey was looking for a source of engines which resulted in a prototype two-seater Nash-Healey being displayed at the London and Paris Auto Salons in 1950. Panelcraft in England built the body, while the chassis was pure Healey, and the engine was a modified Nash Ambassador six-cylinder with a hotter camshaft, aluminum head, and higher compression. US sales began following the Nash-Healey's début at the 1951 Chicago Auto Show. In 1952, Pinin Farina re-styled the Nash-Healey roadster, but sales were still slow. After four years, and a total of only 506 units, the Nash-Healey was dropped from the line-up at the end of 1954. (1953 Nash Healey Le Mans pictured.) (Hyman Ltd Classic Cars)

American Motors

With the formation of American Motors in January 1954 as the fourth largest American automaker, Hudson production was about to be moved to Kenosha. Although Packard refused to join the new venture, it did sign an agreement to sell its V8 engine to AMC. AMC thought in return that Hudson would build Packard bodies, but this failed to happen, and, as a result, AMC rushed to develop its own V8.

In 1954, Hudson models were reworked, with crisper, sharper front end styling, and small rear fins. The Wasp continued in production, but AMC was canceling

For 1955 Hudson Wasp styling was all-new, but based on the big Nash following the merger to form AMC. It featured unique styling for a unique look, whereas the Hudson Metropolitan was pure badge-engineering at its worst. The Hudson Rambler was likewise a thinly disguised Nash. (Courtesy Andrew Mort)

The large door openings on the 1955 Hudson Wasp allowed for easy ingress. The front seats folded flat to line up with the rear and allow for sleeping overnight if traveling long distances on America's new interstate highways. (Courtesy Andrew Mort)

contracts in preparation for its demise. The 1955 Hudsons featured Nash styling and were built in Nash plants in Milwaukee and Kenosha. AMC production rose to 161,792 cars, including 45,535 Hudson badge-engineered cars, of which nearly 20,000 were Hudson Ramblers.

In 1956 Nash, having pioneered the compact car, continued to develop its popular Rambler line-up under AMC management. The Rambler was totally re-designed on the outside. The front end featured a large oval grille housing the headlamps and running lights, set into the fenders. AMC styling director Edmund Anderson added wraparound windscreens which provided the new

It was all style and fashion in the fifties, as seen in this shot of a well-heeled lady and her 1956 Hudson Hornet based on the all-new Rambler. (Courtesy Arthur Caplan)

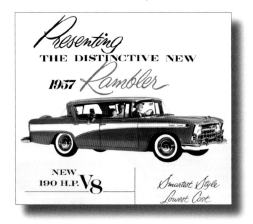

Rambler was a long-term Nash model nameplate and in the early years of the 20th century a marque in its own right. Rambler would become the new AMC division with the disappearance of the Nash and Hudson names in 1958. The stage for this dramatic disappearance of two once very prominent makes was set in 1957 when it became clearly evident that both Hudson and Nash were merely badge-engineered Ramblers. (Author's collection)

Rambler with an airy feel. Large wheel openings, slab sides and special chrome treatments led to three-tone colors. Overall the Rambler had a big car look, yet was a compact, more economical car. At the 1956 Mobilgas Economy Run, the Rambler was placed first overall in gas mileage.

The newly-styled 1956 Rambler was an instant sensation for AMC and production lagged behind demand. In its first year 15,375 Hudson Ramblers were built, while more than twice as many Nash Ramblers were delivered. Total Hudson production was a meager 22,588 cars.

In 1957 both the Nash and Hudson names disappeared in favour of Rambler for 1958. This move and other changes resulted in a $26 million profit after multi-million dollar losses every year since 1954. Production rose from 114,084 cars in 1957 to 199,236 in the 1958 calendar year. AMC was finally firmly established; calendar sales for 1959 topped 400,000 units and surpassed 485,000 in 1960.

1957 was the last year for Hudson models. Dealers stressed the increase in power and decrease in price, but there was also plenty of rather flamboyant style. The 327cu.in (5.4L) V8 was rated at 255hp and mated to Hudson Flashaway Hydra-Matic transmission. Hornet V8 models came in a choice of 32 exterior colors: 15 solid colors, 12 two-tone combinations and 5 custom models in three tones. Production dwindled further from only 10,671 cars in 1956 to just 3876 in 1957.
(Author's collection)

Nash/Hudson/AMC Metropolitan

Well ahead of its time in North America for a volume production sub-compact car was the Nash Metropolitan, powered by an Austin four-cylinder engine. The Nash-Kelvinator Corporation had already been building the Anglo-American Nash-Healey sports car since 1951.

The Metropolitan was based on the original NXI (Nash Experimental International), built on Fiat Topolino mechanicals and the subsequent NKI (Nash-Kelvinator International) prototypes of 1950.

In 1958 AMC had two full lines of Rambler models in two- and four-door sedans and hardtops, as well as wagons. There was the Rambler line and the Rambler American models, which were based on the old Airflyte Rambler Pinin Farina cars. The only non-Rambler model was the Metropolitan, which had appeared in 1954 as a Nash and then a Hudson. It was still in production, and, in fact, the best year for Metropolitan sales was in 1959 when 20,435 units were delivered. This sales total was second only to the Volkswagen Beetle in US imports. Foolishly, AMC would abandon this fast-growing market. By the time production ceased in 1962 a total of 94,986 Metropolitans had been built. (Author's collection)

① Get American big car room and comfort ② Get European small car economy, handling ease

Get the Best of Both—Go Rambler!

See the all-new Rambler with the all-new differences! All-new jet stream styling. All-new Pushbutton transmission with amazing Telovac control! All-new self-cooling brakes. All-new Powr-Lok anti-slip V-8 differential. All-new 100% full-dip rustproofing to keep your Rambler sparkling new much longer. All-new interiors. Airliner Reclining Seats, Twin Travel Beds. Lowest-cost, more efficient All-Season Air Conditioning. See the Rambler that's first in sales gains, first in trade-in value. Be smarter. Buy Rambler and save! *American Motors Means More for Americans*

AT ALL RAMBLER DEALERS

100-INCH WHEELBASE RAMBLER AMERICAN
$1789
Suggested factory delivered price of Rambler American Deluxe at Kenosha, Wisc., including fed. taxes. Flash-O-Matic transmission, white wall tires and other optional equipment, if desired, state and local taxes, if any, extra. *Los Angeles-Miami, with overdrive.

35.39 MILES PER GALLON NASCAR RUN*

The Metropolitan was considered a very small American car, with an 85in wheelbase, a total length of 149.5in, and weighing 1875lb (850kg). Nash thought it would be perfect for capturing a slice of the import market that Austin, Volkswagen and others were competing in. (Courtesy Andrew Mort)

The Metropolitan was built by Fisher and Ludlow Ltd in Britain and shipped to the Austin, Longbridge plant for assembly, before being exported to America. It was introduced in March 1954, shortly before the AMC Nash-Hudson merge, in Hardtop ($1445) or Convertible ($1469) form. The Metropolitan wore a Nash badge, but soon after the merger Hudson versions appeared (1954-56). By 1956 AMC decided to refer to the car simply as a Metropolitan.

The Metropolitan was first powered by an Austin 42hp, 73cu.in (1.2L), four-cylinder engine, but in 1956 was upgraded with a larger 52hp, 92cu.in (1.5L) engine (1956-62) providing a top speed of 78mph (126kph).

The diminutive Metropolitan's styling cues and overall lines were borrowed from the larger car lines built by Nash, yet the little Metropolitan was built by Fisher and Ludlow Ltd in Britain and then shipped to the Austin, Longbridge plant for assembly, before being exported to America. (Courtesy Andrew Mort)

Only basic instrumentation was offered in the Austin-built and powered Metropolitan. The shifter emerged from a ball-joint connection where the steering wheel and dash panel met. (Courtesy Andrew Mort)

Willys & Kaiser-Willys

Willys-Overland was established as a car maker in Toledo, Ohio in 1908 following the takeover of the Overland automobile company (est. 1905), and the Standard Wheel Company (est. 1903).

Although headed by former car dealer John North Willys, the Willys name temporarily disappeared by 1910, while the Overland brand continued. It was the second best selling automobile maker behind Ford by 1915. The Overland line of cars was selling well, as were the various lesser-known brands in the group, such as the Marion and the smaller Willys-Knight powered by a double sleeve-valve engine.

1928 proved to be a record year for Willys-Overland with more than 231,000 units being built. John North Willys turned over the company to his vice-president in 1929, and was appointed the first American Ambassador to Poland in 1930.

The company's fortunes changed dramatically after the great stock market crash and by 1933 the company was forced into receivership. John North Willys returned to take control of his failing company at the

During WWII newspaper advertisements, such as this dramatic combat situation, left an indelible impression of the Jeep in the eyes of the American public. (Author's collection)

A true incident from the battle at B

THE SUN NEVER SETS ON THE MIGHTY JEEP

SIGNAL CORPS UNIT BEATS RING OF DEATH

IN JEEPS FROM WILLYS-OVERLAND

Lieutenant . . . ., U. S. Army Signal Corps, as a alt of the following exploit during the victorious re on Bizerte, was "awarded the Silver Star for antry in action, outstanding leadership, courage and iative." His report states:

☆   ☆   ☆

ur post was right up there in the front line—and our was to keep communications open between staff dquarters and the units in action.

We were damned short of transportation vehicles, with three tough little Jeeps and a couple of trucks had fought our way up front to S—— through an y blackout and a mass of traffic the night before— sday.

At about 1900 hours (7 P.M.) on Wednesday night, avy artillery duel could be plainly heard from our ssage center. Bombing and strafing were continuous. e wire layers and repair crews were under enemy fire the time—but we kept the lines open.

Then reports coming through showed things weren't ng so good out there. It looked like our little town

of S—— might be encircled, and us with it, at any moment.

"At about 2100 hours (9 P.M.) some French soldiers came to us for hand grenades to blow up the civilian switchboard they had been operating and to go out with us when we left.

"But our Corps Signal Officer told them to put the switchboard out on the sidewalk and that we would pick it up when and *if* we left.

Things got worse out there so I sent most of our wire crews and messengers back. Just enough of us stayed on to keep the message center going.

"We had just started to cut our circuits when an ammunition dump about a hundred yards from us blew up with a loud roar, showering us with sparks and shrapnel. We thought we had caught a direct bomb hit. But when we found out what it really was we kept right on working.

"Finally, at about 0300 hours (3 A.M.), we completed our cutover and were loaded to pull out. We gave our over-burdened Jeeps the gun and they got going. As we left, the whole sky was aflame, and the ammunition

dump continued to explode. We were s rounded that we could hear the machine a few hundred yards away.

"It was up to the Jeeps to take us thro gap left in that ring of death. As we ca French Telephone Co. building we saw the on the sidewalk. We loaded it on the hoo and, with this added burden, we beat it through a veritable inferno.

"It was nip and tuck all the way, and if failed us, even for a moment, our goose been cooked. But they didn't fail and we ar quarters, back of the lines, about 0445 hours with all of our equipment and personnel an casualties."

☆   ☆   ☆

It is *our* great privilege in this war to suppl built Jeeps that are today serving thousan American and other United Nations fight every battle front in the world, and in ev moving invasion. Willys-Overland Motor

WILLYS

JEEPS, MOTOR CARS AND TRUCKS

The fighting heart of every Jeep in the world— the source of its amazing power, speed, flexi dependability and fuel economy—is the Jeep Devil" Engine, which was designed and perf by Willys-Overland.

behest of President Hoover, and felt the low price field was what the company needed to focus on to survive.

By 1936 the company was back on its feet, but the strain had proven too much for the aging John North Willys, who had died from a heart attack at the end of 1935.

Then out of receivership, Willys survived the decade, going through various model name changes again to become known as Willys-Americar in 1940.

During WWII Willys-Overland and Ford built American Jeeps for the military. When production resumed in 1945 Willys added a civilian model to the

Although very utilitarian, the Jeep Station Wagon could be ordered with a stylish faux 'woody' look, which was very popular at this time with film stars and the country set. (Author's collection)

Jeep line-up known as the CJ, and sold licenses to Hotchkiss in France, Mitsubishi in Japan, and others.

The civilian-made CJ Jeeps were slightly more sophisticated than the military versions, and were soon offered in many other guises, starting in 1946, for everything from farming to fire fighting. In addition to these models, a Jeep-based 1-ton pickup and stake truck was introduced in 2X4 and 4X4 form in 1947.

Although more truck-like than automobile, a very utilitarian station wagon could be ordered in faux painted 'woody' form in 2X4 and, by 1949, 4X4 versions. These

models, plus even more variations of the CJ Jeep, were offered throughout the 1950s and into the 1960s.

Somewhat more car-like was the Jeepster, which entered production on April 3rd 1948 and remained in production until 1950, although approximately 2000 unsold units found owners as 1951 models. Designed by famed Brook Stevens, who had also designed the Jeep pickup and station wagon, the Jeepster was still unmistakably a Jeep, but had far sportier lines, sat lower, and was even more civilized. The two-door Jeepster was offered in stylish Phaeton form and had the distinction

The sportier four-seater Jeepster Phaeton with its more luxurious interior was built on the same frame as the more mundane station wagon. Available only as a 2X4, its sporty car looks, including cut-down doors, belied the fact it weighed in at a hefty 2556lb (1159kg) and was powered by a 134.2cu.in (2.2L), 63hp, four-cylinder engine. The 1950-51 models can be identified by the horizontal rather than vertical grille treatment and the more powerful 72hp, F-head four-cylinder engine.
(Author's collection)

The gas cap on the Aero was placed in the centre at the back, just below the trunk lid that allowed for easier fuel fill-ups regardless of what side of the pump island you were on. The license plate light illuminated the opening for night fillings. It was a fairly novel feature at this time. (Courtesy Andrew Mort)

of being the last Phaeton built in the United States. Its best year was 1948 when a total of 10,362 four-cylinder Jeepsters were sold. The 70hp, 148cu.in (2.4L) L-head six-cylinder engine was offered as an option in 1949 for those looking for a bit more power.

In 1952, as Jeep sales faltered, Willys re-entered the car market after an absence of ten years with its

The more expensive Aero-Ace was immediately identifiable by its wraparound rear windscreen. All Aero models featured what Willys called 'Aeroframe Construction.' Apparently, "… engineers threw away the old-fashioned underframe and came up with a car whose body and chassis are welded together into one extra strong, rigid unit – providing greater passenger safety – eliminating a large amount of needless fuel-wasting weight.' (Author's collection)

The shape of the unibody design of the Aero was subtle, yet stylish, but moreover very practical as the driver was able to see all four corners of the car without strain when parking. And pointed out in brochures, "… the sloping plane-wing hood lets you see the road only 10ft (3m) ahead of your bumper." (Courtesy Andrew Mort)

The Aero was 72in wide and stood 60in tall on 4.50 X 15 wheels, with a turning circle of 37.9ft (12m). (Courtesy Andrew Mort)

The Aero was often described as being the compact car with a big car interior. The front and rear seats were 61in wide, with 35½in of headroom in front and just 1in less in the rear, yet the wheelbase was only 108in with an overall length of 180in. (Courtesy Andrew Mort)

compact Aero. Although advertised as an economical 'compact' car, the Aero could comfortably sit three abreast on its front and rear bench seats, and deliver excellent fuel economy. Originally, the Aero was available

Another feature of the compact Aero was its tasteful, comfortable, yet well-equipped interior. The dashboard featured full instrumentation and a bin-type glove compartment on the right side. Warning lights were used for the oil pressure and ammeter readings.
(Courtesy Andrew Mort)

By 1953 the Aero was available with a choice of two six-cylinder engines. The standard engine was the 90hp, 161cu.in (2.6L), F-head capable of moving the Aero 0-50mph (0-80kph) in just 11 seconds. In comparison, a Ford V8 in 1952 was rated at 100hp.
(Courtesy Andrew Mort)

only as a two-door sedan in two very distinct models. The Aero Wing had a more formal roofline, while the Aero Ace, with its wraparound three-piece rear windscreen, featured an almost panoramic view of the road. Total Aero production in both six-cylinder models totaled 31,363 units in 1952.

By 1953 the Aero line-up had been expanded and featured two new body styles; a four-door sedan and an exclusive two-door hardtop.

Top-of-the-line was the stylish Aero-Eagle two-door hardtop powered by the Hurricane 6 engine. The gold-plated 'W' on the grille signified Willys-Overland's fiftieth Anniversary. The Aero-Wing was replaced by the Aero-Falcon powered by the more economical Lightning Six.

There was also nothing compact about the Aero trunk; the squared-off dimensions allowed for a family load of typical 1950s hard-sided luggage. (Courtesy Andrew Mort)

Willys was proud of its 'Color-Symphony Interiors.' As the 1953 brochure pointed out, "Step into luxury … for the color-ensemble interiors of the Aero Willys are truly luxurious. You'll sit into soft, cushioned seats formed to give you restful, natural support. Here is the interior … showing the easy-to-see instrument grouping and the smart upholstery, trimmed in colors to harmonize with exterior body color." (Courtesy Andrew Mort)

The base model was the Aero-Lark DeLuxe, while the top-of-the-line sedan model continued to be the Aero-Ace with its unique roofline and more powerful Hurricane 6 engine. These models were available only in sedan form. Production increased in 1953 to 41,375 units.

By 1953, all the Frazer models had disappeared and Kaiser was looking to find another company to help expand his car line-up to compete with the Big Three. Thus, in the spring of 1953 Kaiser took control of Willys-Overland.

The Willys Aero and similarly sized and marketed Henry J, along with the face-lifted, full-size Kaiser, became the new line-up for 1954.

The least expensive model in the 1954 K-W line-up was the very basic Aero-Lark four-cylinder model, sans

Fuel mileage was sensational for a six, with an average of 35mpg (based on US gallons). How much of this was due to aerodynamic design is questionable, but the Aero was consistently pictured at airport settings. Then there was its jet-like hood ornament penned by none other than William Mitchell.
(Courtesy Andrew Mort)

Although most Aero Willys built were powered by six-cylinder engines, a four-cylinder model known as the Lark DeLuxe was added in 1954.
(Courtesy Andrew Mort)

brightwork trim along with other niceties to cut costs. The Lark was also offered with the 161cu.in (2.6L) Lightning F-head, six-cylinder engine. The Kaiser 115hp, 226cu. in (3.7L) L-head engine became the big six in the higher priced Aero models, but could also be ordered even in the Lark. The moving of Kaiser production to Toledo from the old Willow plant was in part responsible for Aero-Willys production dropping to a meager 11,865 cars.

For 1955 the Aero was given a mild facelift, featuring a Kaiser-like grille, different taillights and side trim. The Aero name disappeared with just the Ace (soon renamed the Custom), and the Bermuda (originally named Eagle) designation being marketed. The once top-of-the-line two-door hardtop became 'America's lowest priced hardtop!' at $1895.

Corporate decisions and minimal sales saw the Willys Aero tooling crated and sent to Kaiser Industries in Brazil where it found a new market and was built in only slightly different form through to 1962.

American Jeep production continued and, although controlled by Kaiser, the Willys-Overland Company continued in name and was initially a separate entity. In 1963, Willys-Overland became the Kaiser-Jeep Corporation.

THE *Aero* WILLYS *"Eagle Custom"*

The Willys Aero Eagle Custom was the ultimate model in the line-up with its continental tire. (Author's collection)

The overall dimensions of the compact Willys Aero compared very favourably with its larger competition. Although the full-size 1952 Ford was nearly 16in longer and almost 5in taller, the Aero was just under an inch wider. (Courtesy Andrew Mort)

The Aero-Eagle

THE AERO-EAGLE . . . the airiness of a dashing convertible with closed-car protection . . . powered by the high-compression *HURRICANE 6 Engine.* The big one-piece windshield, wrap-around rear window and completely open sides give a control-tower view of out-of-doors. Yet, in but a moment, you close the windows against the elements and ride in snug comfort. It's a sports car . . . it's a family car . . . the Aero-Eagle, a truly great car. For advanced styling, probably no other American motor car has won the acceptance and praises accorded this new car.

The two-door hardtop was by far the most attractive Willys, albeit the most expensive model offered in the Aero line-up. The Eagle was described as a 'hardtop convertible' due to its overall look. The Eagle would be renamed the Bermuda in 1955, but just over 2000 were sold before production was halted in June. Total Willys car production in 1955 reached 6564 units. The total Willys Aero models for all years built was 92,046 units. (Author's collection)

The Lark DeLuxe was the base Aero model in 1954, and was most often powered by the F-head, 90hp, six-cylinder engine. (Courtesy Andrew Mort)

Styling nuances such as the delicate, jewel-like design of the Willys Aero rear taillight set it apart from the other mass-produced models of the 1950s. (Courtesy Andrew Mort)

Crosley, Checker & Tucker

Crosley – 'The Car of Tomorrow'

Powel Crosley Jr had been immensely successful at whatever he had attempted. He was an inventor who began his fascination with automobiles when he was a boy. At age fourteen he built himself an electric car, but Crosley would not become known for his automobile until much later. Over the ensuing years there would be many other non-automotive designs and products bearing the Crosley name.

After working at everything, from selling door-to-door to repairing telephones, Crosley and a partner started a mail order advertising business. By 1920 Crosley was sole owner and taking in over a million dollars a year.

After his son asked for a radio, Crosley approached the University of Cincinnati and formed a team of undergraduate students to develop a low-cost model. His bargain radios were an overnight success and by 1922 Crosley was the world's largest manufacturer. Crosley then entered into radio broadcasting and established 'The Nation's Station' based in Cincinnati.

Further success resulted in Crosley building kitchen appliances, and he owned the patent for shelves in refrigerator doors. A keen sportsman, Crosley added the Cincinnati Reds (1934) to the Crosley Radio Corporation. Despite his Cinci mansion, country homes in various states and Canada, a hundred foot yacht, and a Duesenberg, Crosley still wanted to fulfill his boyhood dream of building automobiles.

On April 29th 1939, at the Indianapolis Speedway, Crosley introduced his rudimentary lightweight 'Car of Tomorrow.' Here was an Austin Seven-sized car priced at just over $300 for the depression-weary public.

The Crosley's proprietary engine was built by the Waukesha Motor Company of Wisconsin, which had originally designed the unit for powering an orchard sprayer.

Crosleys were sold via 200 dealers or any store that carried Crosley appliances, yet despite nation-wide publicity, sales were barely keeping the factory going in 1940 as production dipped to 422 units.

Part of the problem was the durability of its powertrain – the solution was a reduction in engine displacement and the use of universal joints. Sales rose steadily to 2289 units in 1941, and quickly to over 1000 in early 1942, before production was halted when America entered WWII later that year.

Following WWII, the Crosley re-appeared powered by the 44cu.in (721cc), copper brazed Cobra four-cylinder unit boasting 26.5hp @ 5000rpm. Fresh post-war styling heavily influenced by Powel Crosley saw the overall length reduced by nearly 13in, and the door handles mounted at different heights in order to ship the cars side-by-side in boxcars.

Initially only a sedan was offered, but a convertible and pickup were added as the first post-war sales year ended. Although production never reached the levels Crosley had predicted, the company prospered despite the steel shortages and strikes that were common in those early post-war years. In fact, the first 5000 cars off the line had no badges and the Crosley name was painted on the bumper.

Total production in 1947 exceeded 19,000 and rose to 28,734 in 1948, which included an industry high number of approximately 20,000 station wagons.

BELOW ... STANDARD BUSINESS COUPE 2 passenger with big luggage space back of the front seats. Will carry ¼ ton of sample cases, merchandise, baggage. Sliding windows. An ideal car for the traveling man. Parks where other cars can't. Holds down expenses by delivering 35 to 50 miles on a gallon of regular gasoline.

BELOW ... SUPER SPORTS Super edition of the Hotshot, now with solid, hinged doors. Also has folding top, zipper side curtains, complete plastic leather cockpit edge trim and liner, matching the red upholstery.

The post-war Crosley models were powered by a four-cylinder, water-cooled, 26.5hp, 44cu.in (0.72L) Cobra engine capable of 80mph (50kph). The Crosley had a wheelbase of 80in, an overall length of 145in, and a total weight of 1150lb (68kg).
(Author's collection)

The plant was expanded by forty per cent, but a problem emerged. The unique sheet metal Cobra engine that had proven reliable in combat situations had a major design failure. Although dependable, it was never tested over a long period of time and an impending electrolysis problem had not been foreseen. Word of the engine defect, combined with an increasingly larger number of full-size secondhand cars, resulted in a dramatic decline in sales.

For 1949 a new engine was designed, known as CIBA (Cast Iron Block Assembly) it was installed in a re-styled model line-up. The new Crosley models were the first American cars equipped with four-wheel disc brakes.

The sports car craze had not gone unnoticed and Crosley introduced the two-seater Hotshot. Production was disappointing and only 752 were sold, despite its 0-50mph (80kph) time of 25 seconds and top speed of 82mph (125kph). Total 1949 Crosley production was below 8000 units.

Sales continued to tumble, and in 1950 the disc brakes were replaced by drums after road salt began causing problems.

In 1951 the Crosley line saw further refinement, but sales now averaged only 6000 units.

THREE PACE-SETTING MODELS IN AUTOMOBILE HISTORY!

These three photos dramatically demonstrate the tremendous changes in the Crosley from 1938 to 1949. The pictures were taken on the same day, in exactly the same place without moving the camera.

TODAY

CROSLEY MOTORS, INC.,
2532 Spring Grove Ave.,
Cincinnati 14, Ohio

PRINTED IN U.S.A.

1938 The lowest-priced quantity-produced American car ever sold in the U. S. $350 F.O.B., Richmond, Indiana.

1947 The first post-war Crosley that swept the field at less than the cost of an 8-year-old high-upkeep used car.

One of the reasons for the initial success of the 1947 Crosley was the fact that this brand-new two-door sedan cost less than an 8-year old used car. (Author's collection)

Finally in May 1952, after putting over $3 million of his personal funds in the company, Crosley decided to halt production. The car company was eventually acquired by General Tire and Rubber in July 1952 at 20 cents a share. General Tire and Rubber then merged with Aerojet, and the Crosley factory was outfitted for the production of rocket parts.

Checker – from taxi to family car

Established by Morris Markin, Checker Motors Corporation of Kalamazoo, Michigan began building taxi cabs in 1923, and in 1933 had become part of E L Cord's conglomerate that included production of Auburn, Cord and Duesenberg cars. In 1936, Cord sold his holdings in Checker back to Markin. Both would soon be investigated for stock manipulation.

A re-designed version of Checker's popular, spacious taxicab appeared in 1947. In styling the post-war Checker looked very much like the carried-over GM cars, and could be ordered as a private 'pleasure car' for the first time from 1948. Buses as well as taxicabs were being built at this time, but Checker would soon focus chiefly on taxicabs.

By 1954 it became apparent that a more modern looking Checker was needed, and so, in preparation, production stopped for over nine months.

To increase production and broaden its market, Checker introduced its first year non-commercial models in 1959. Production increased to 1050 vehicles, and in 1960 it would more than double. (Author's collection)

Unveiled late in 1955, full production of the more contemporary-looking, full frame, Continental Six-cylinder Checker A-8 didn't commence until 1956. Although priced lower than the former model, it was still more expensive than the slightly smaller, more economical Plymouth with the Chrysler taxicab package.

A mild re-designed Checker was introduced in October 1958, featuring quad headlamps, a wraparound rear window, a new grille, plus some new engine and power options.

At this time, passenger car models were announced in 4-door sedan, station wagon (introduced in 1960), and as stretch limousines. All Checkers provided seating for eight, thanks to folding jump seats in the back, while the limousines accommodated nine, or twelve in six-door format. Options to make these cars less spartan included: power brakes; power steering; a power seat; an automatic transmission; and a more powerful 140hp, Continental Six-cylinder engine.

Production of the non-commercial Checker models officially began in June 1959, but a strike and lack of dealers resulted in a delayed 'official launch' of the new Superba until December 1959.

Whereas, a 1952 survey discovered 9055 operators

out of a total of 11,787 licensed taxicab drivers in New York drove Checker cabs, by 1962 that number had shrunk to around 2000 due to increased competition from the Big Three.

Checker was one of the first American automobiles to be offered with a diesel engine in 1968. Despite this, and attempting to build niche custom models and limos, the last Checker rolled off the assembly line on July 12th 1982.

Tucker – Setting a new pattern of safety

WWII had proven to be profitable for many industrialists, yet in peacetime had resulted in a large number of factories left idle. Preston Tucker made his initial fortune through Tucker Tool and Dye based in Ypsilanti, Michigan. Established in 1946, The Tucker Corporation of Chicago planned to build a sports car, but this soon evolved into the novel Alex Tremulis-designed four-door sedan. As well as being mechanically very innovative, the Tucker was designed with safety in mind. Early advertisements stressed its disc brakes, sponge rubber padded dash crash cowl, front seat safety compartment engineering, pop-out safety glass windscreen, the added centre turning headlamp known as the 'Tucker Cyclops Eye,' rear-mounted engine for overall balanced weight distribution, no engine heat or fumes inside the car, the ability of the front seat passenger to drop under the cowl into a steel re-enforced 'Crash Chamber' for added protection in a front end collision, and a safety frame design to protect passengers in accidents.

Quite revolutionary in its design, production delays and a court battle initiated by the Securities Exchange Commission, which charged Tucker with fraud and violations, resulted in only forty-nine cars being built. Tucker was found not guilty in 1950, but had spent most of his fortune defending himself. In 1954 he once again attempted to build another car, but this time in Brazil. Unfortunately, that plan ended with his death in 1956.

An early advertisement stressed Tucker safety and brought a 'Progress Report from the Tucker Plant,' which stated, "Already the first fleet of pilot cars is being produced. Production lines are being set up. In a matter of months you'll see Tucker '48s on the road." The Tucker weighed 3600lb (1633kg) and had a turning radius of only 10ft 8in. The just over 60in tall Tucker was powered by a Franklin six-cylinder engine used in helicopters – originally air-cooled, Tucker converted the engine to water-cooled for its cars. (Author's collection)

Great ideas, great failures

The post-WWII boom brought with it the hopes and dreams of many to build a new kind of American car. Stylish sports cars were particularly popular thanks to British and European influences, and it was in this area that numerous American entrepreneurs, designers and sportsmen shone in new and daring designs. Glasspar, Woodill, Darrin, Kurtis, Muntz and others introduced very different, often exciting cars in the 1950s, although some, in hindsight, were foolish follies. There were literally dozens, but here are a few of the more prominent makes.

Cunningham (1951-1955)
American Briggs Cunningham competed at Le Mans in 1950 with his Le Monstre Cadillacs and finished 10th and 11th. He then set out to build the C-1 prototype, which evolved into the C-2, as an American production sports racing car. After designing and racing the C-2 in America in order to qualify as a manufacturer, Cunningham had to build production cars. In 1952 a Cunningham C-3 chassis was built in West Palm Beach and then shipped to Italy where Vignale fitted the Michelotti-styled coachwork. The 331cu.in (5.4L) Chrysler V8 which powered the race cars sat in a chassis featuring an independent front suspension, live rear axle, coil springs, hydraulic shock absorbers and Mercury drum brakes. At the same time, the C-4R evolved and was built for racing. It successfully competed at Le Mans in 1952 and then in 1953, finishing 3rd and 5th which were Cunningham's best race results. On the production side, only 30 examples of the C-3 sports car were built, of which 26 were coupes.
(Author's collection)

Darrin (1955-1958)

With the end of car production at Kaiser, Howard 'Dutch' Darrin took his sports car and attempted to market it himself. Approximately 100 uncompleted cars were sold with supercharged Willys and Cadillac engines.

Dual-Ghia (1956-1958)

Dual-Ghia is best remembered as the car of the famous American 'Rat Pack.' Dual-Ghias were owned by Frank Sinatra, Dean Martin, and others in this exclusive band of friends. Lucile Ball, Hoagy Carmichael and composer David Rose also owned these stylish cars. Created by Gene Casaroll of Detroit, whose Dual Motors had built trucks, the Ghia was based on the 1954 Virgil Exner Dodge Firearrow IV show car. Having purchased the rights, fellow Detroit car man Paul Farago, who was the Ghia rep in the US, did some re-design work on this heavily Chrysler-based four-seater. Approximately 100 were built from 1956-58. A further marketing attempt was made from 1960-62, but few were built. (1957 Dual Ghia pictured.) (Courtesy Hyman Motors Ltd)

Davis (1947-1949)

The Davis was a definite folly. Only 17 of this 3-wheel, four abreast single benchseat, four-cylinder engine, bullet-shaped cars were built.

Edwards America (1953-55)
West Coast industrialist Sterling Edwards competed in early road races in California in a car of his own design. Edwards went on to build a two-seater, fiberglass-bodied sports car called the Edwards America. Based on the Henry J frame and powered by an Oldsmobile V8, just five were built, of which only two were convertibles. (1954 Edwards America pictured.)
(Courtesy Hyman Motors Ltd)

Excalibur (1952-1975)

The designer Brooks Stevens created an Allard J2-like, two-seater built on a Henry J chassis and powered by the Willys 2.6L six-cylinder engine. The original was campaigned in the US where it beat Jaguars and Ferraris. Only four were built in 1952-53, but a later 1958 envelope-bodied Excalibur won the SCCA Championship. In 1964 Stevens began building an M-B SSK-looking replica which, despite its high cost, found celebrity status, and many buyers, including Steve McQueen, Liberace, George Foreman, Rod Stewart, Prince Rainier, Arnold Schwarzenegger, and dozens more. Both two-seaters, and later four-seaters, were powered by a Corvette V8 engine, although the originals were fitted with Studebaker V8s. Production ended in 1988.

Flajole (1955)

Automobile designer Bill Flajole (Chrysler, General Motors, Ford and Nash) decided to create his own American version of a European sports car, based on a Jaguar XK120 wheelbase and powered by its six-cylinder DOHC engine. The Flajole Forerunner was a fiberglass two-seater, which featured an innovative retractable translucent roof panel that slid-away out-of-sight. Only one was built, reportedly used by its builder as daily transportation into the 1970s.
(Courtesy Hyman Motors Ltd)

The 1950s was a very creative and innovative period in automotive design. While some concepts, such as the Flajole exterior rearview mirror, never saw production, eventually the disappearing glass top, glass T-Bar roof panels, safer high-back bucket seats and folding hardtops would become incorporated into models decades later. (Courtesy Hyman Motors)

Muntz (1951-1954)

In 1947 Earl 'Mad Man' Muntz, as he was known for his crazy sales pitches, sold television sets, stereo tape decks, radios, motor homes, and $72 million in new and used cars. Muntz bought two Kurtis sports cars designed by Frank Kurtis and loved them so much that he decided to buy the rights and began production in 1951 as the Muntz Car Co of Evanston, Illinois. After the first 28 cars built, Muntz switched from Cadillac engines to a standard Lincoln V8. In 1953 there were few styling changes, but the Muntz body switched from aluminum to steel. There was a 260lb weight increase, as well as an increase in the price to $5114. Muntz production is estimated from as few as 200 units to as many as 400 units. A Muntz Jet was a very special car in 1953, which appealed to numerous wealthy entrepreneurs and celebrities.

King Midget (1947-1969)

The King Midget was true to its name. This 8½hp or later 9½hp micro vehicle was more golf cart than automobile. Few ventured out on real roads. Everything was optional, including doors, a top, and even a speedometer. About 5000 were built.

Kurtis (1949-1955)

Frank Kurtis was a highly successful race car builder in America, but his attempts at production sports cars failed to make any impact. His original show car-based model was sold to Muntz after just 34 were built. His first generation 500 models – a sort of American Allard J2 in concept – ceased production after only 52 were completed, and his envelope-bodied 500M disappeared after just 24 were made.

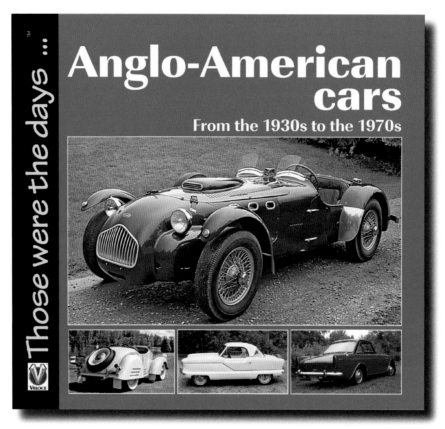

Anglo-American cars
From the 1930s to the 1970s

Those were the days ...

Covers British cars powered by American engines and American cars fitted with British power plants, all built from the 1930s to the 1970s. The first book dedicated solely to these unique hybrids bearing both American and British engineering, made for those who lust to drive something different.

£14.99
ISBN: 978-1-845842-33-8

For more info on Veloce titles, visit our website at www.veloce.co.uk
email info@veloce.co.uk • tel: +44 (0)1305 260068 • prices subject to change • p+p extra

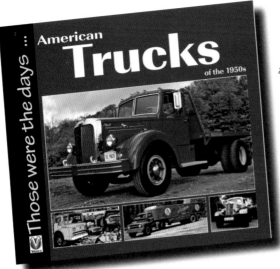

This highly visual study examines the important role of trucks and trucking in the 1950s, recounting the essential role they played in the industrial growth of the US and Canada. Features factory photos, advertisements, original truck brochures and restored examples, plus a comprehensive guide to all models produced.

£14.99
ISBN: 978-1-845842-27-7

This highly visual study examines the important role of trucking in the growth of North America in the 1960s, when stiff competition led to failures and mergers. Features factory photos, advertisements, original brochures and restored examples, plus a comprehensive guide of all models produced.

£14.99
ISBN: 978-1-845842-28-4

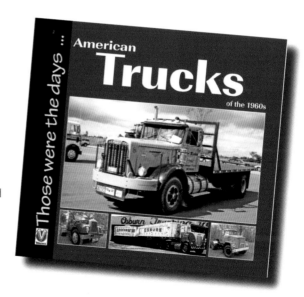

For more info on Veloce titles, visit our website at www.veloce.co.uk
email info@veloce.co.uk • tel: +44 (0)1305 260068 • prices subject to change • p+p extra

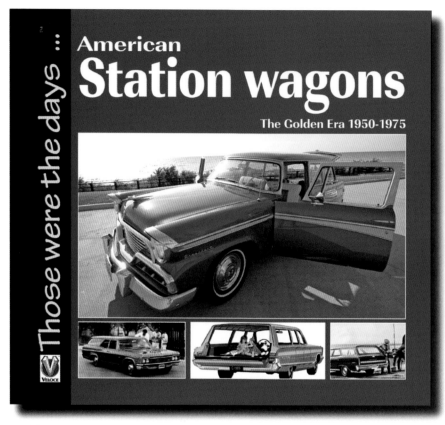

This book examines the important quarter century period when the American station wagon was a family standard and status symbol of a successful suburban lifestyle, recounting its essential role in North American society in the 1950s, 1960s and 1970s.

£14.99
ISBN: 978-1-845842-68-0

For more info on Veloce titles, visit our website at www.veloce.co.uk
email info@veloce.co.uk • tel: +44 (0)1305 260068 • prices subject to change • p+p extra

Index

Index